"I write from the most comfortable quarters I have ever had in the United States... in the house of my friend Andrew Low of the great house of A. Low and Co., cotton dealers, brokers, merchants."

—William Makepeace Thackeray
from a letter published 1856,
Thackeray in the United States

The
ANDREW LOW
HOUSE

Tania June Sammons

TANIA JUNE SAMMONS

with

VIRGINIA CONNERAT LOGAN

Enjoy!

The National Society of The Colonial Dames
of America in the State of Georgia

The University of Georgia Press   Athens

GEORGIA

Entrusted With History's Future

Donors

Foreword

I am proud and happy to present this book, marking the 90th year that The National Society of The Colonial Dames of America in the State of Georgia has owned and maintained the historic Andrew Low House in Savannah, Georgia. With the publication of *The Andrew Low House* anniversary book in 2018 we also mark the 125th Anniversary of the founding of the Georgia Society in 1893.

The Andrew Low House, constructed in 1848, is one of the gems of the National Landmark Historic District in Savannah. The house and garden, the lives of its famous owners, and its unrivaled decorative arts collection has garnered the attention of historians and antiquarians around the world, not to mention welcoming nearly 85,000 visitors annually, as well as serving as headquarters for 1,600 Georgia Dames.

The preservation of silver, porcelain, art and archival materials in the museum collection distinguishes it as an important part of Georgia history. The period furnishings which are documented room by room include works by some of America's most prestigious furniture makers.

The original concept for this book began years ago as the brainchild of Virginia Connerat Logan, whose manuscript, *Andrew Low's Legacy*, was published most recently in 2016. Characters, events, and folklore from Mrs. Logan's research delightfully enrich the text of this volume. It should also be noted that the J. Robert Logan, Jr. Foundation provided the means to launch this cherished publication.

Tania June Sammons, co-author of *The Andrew Low House*, has written a rich and detailed overview of the people and the collection, working with renowned photographer Richard Leo Johnson, who produced the beautiful photographs of the artifacts and grounds that are featured within these pages.

This 90th anniversary book is the 125th Celebration project of the Savannah Town Committee, who contributed a large portion of the funds to produce this volume. The photography was funded by a grant from the NSCDA-GA Ways and Means Committee.

In its truest sense, the Andrew Low House story has been written by all the Dames who have loved and cared for our wonderful edifice over the 90 years we have been its caretakers.

It is a high honor to tell readers about the meaning and purpose of our organization, which is dedicated to keeping patriotism and history alive for generations to come. Our Andrew Low House is the landmark though which we serve this purpose.

—Joy Daniels Schwartz, NSCDA-GA President, 2016–2019

Contents

Introduction

The Andrew Low House

℘⁖ Although named for one man, the Andrew
Low House has served as a home, workplace, headquarters, and tourist destination for people of all
backgrounds for nearly 150 years. Andrew Low, his
family, and free and enslaved servants first inhabited
the house in the mid-nineteenth century. In the
early twentieth century, Girl Scout founder Juliette
"Daisy" Gordon Low lived in the dwelling and used
the carriage house for Girl Scout meetings. In
1928, The National Society of The Colonial Dames
of America in the State of Georgia purchased the
home from the estate of Juliette Gordon Low to use
as their headquarters. Today, the Georgia Dames
share the site as a historic house museum with more
than 80,000 domestic and international visitors
each year.

The People

Andrew Low and Family

〰️ Born in Kincardinshire County, Scotland, in 1812, Andrew Low immigrated to Savannah in 1829, at the age of seventeen. Andrew Low worked for his uncle and namesake, to whom he quickly demonstrated his worth. Eventually the younger Andrew Low inherited his uncle's dry goods and cotton factorage businesses in Savannah and Liverpool. Both Lows often held partnerships with other men, including family members. In 1844, Andrew Low married his first wife, Sarah Cecil Hunter (1817–1849). A friend described Sarah Low as "a remarkably happy amiable and rational character." The couple swiftly added three children to their family: Andrew (1844–1848), Amy (1846–1917), and Harriet "Hattie" (1847–1891). In 1848, their son Andrew died at age four. The following year, Sarah Low died after a miscarriage. After her death, Sarah's sister Elizabeth Hunter moved in with the family to help care for the children and manage the home. She lived with them for three years.

In 1854, Andrew Low married his second wife Mary Cowper Stiles (1832–1863). Mary's niece noted her aunt's beauty, but also recognized that she "was a genuine out-door girl, who is said to ride and

Portrait of Andrew Low, 1836, by George Washington Conarroe.

Portrait of Sarah Cecil Hunter Low and daughter Amy, 1849, by C. Durham.

shoot even better than her brothers." Andrew and Mary lived an active life that involved multiple overseas trips, including an 1861 mission to England on behalf of the Confederacy. The Lows actively assisted in plans and funding, and Mary even carried copies of secret documents in her clothing on her return trip. She escaped arrest, but her husband, his former partner Charles Green, and Green's sister Eliza Green Low (also the widow of Andrew's cousin John), spent time in Union prisons.

During Mary and Andrew Low's nine years together the couple had six children, four of whom survived: Katherine "Katie" Mackay (1855–1923), Mary (1859–1932), William "Willie" Mackay (1860–1905), and Jessie (1862–1934). The Lows shared a happy life, but, like Sarah Low, Mary succumbed to pregnancy complications and died in 1863. For a second time in Andrew Low's life his wife's relative moved into the home for three years to help care for the children and the house. This time, Mary's mother Eliza Mackay Stiles (1809–1867) joined the family.

After the Civil War, in 1867, Andrew Low moved his family to Leamington Spa, England. From this point forward Andrew Low spent most of his time abroad, but traveled once a year, during the winter months, to Savannah. Low died in England in 1886. Later that year his family returned his remains to Savannah where he was buried at Laurel Grove Cemetery. According to the *Savannah Morning News*, Low's personal estate totaled approximately 617,000 pounds. Each of his daughters received 70,000 pounds, which included a gift of 10,000 pounds from

Portrait of Mary Cowper Stiles as a teenager, possibly painted by her mother Eliza Mackay Stiles.

Portrait of Mary Cowper Stiles Low, 1854, by unknown artist.

their brother William. Andrew Low's only son received the residual of his father's estate. Low also left bequests to the Union Society, the Episcopal Orphan's Home (Bethesda), the Widow's Society, the Female Orphan Asylum, and the sisters of Mercy for the Catholic Female Orphan Asylum, all in Savannah. He also bequeathed an annual sum of $300 to Tom Milledge, but his Savannah butler had already preceded him in death.

Andrew Low's children, from left to right in back row: Hattie, Jeesie, Katie, Willie, and Amy. Seated in the front: Mary.

Portrait of Jessie Low Graham, youngest child of Andrew and Mary Low, c. 1895, attributed to Charles Alexander.

Free and Enslaved Servants

᠅ Census records, tax digests, deeds, letters, and Savannah's Registers of Free People of Color, provide clues to how Andrew Low managed his home with both enslaved and free people. The 1850 U.S. Census records the free inhabitants of the house as Low, his two daughters, and sister-in-law. The enslaved staff included six black men, ages 24–60, and five women, ages 31–50. Three of the women are listed as "black," and two are listed as "mulatto," a term used to reference a person of mixed race. Instead of listing the names of the enslaved individuals as recorded on the free inhabitants schedule, the slave inhabitants document only notes the name of their owner.

Ten years later, in 1860, the U.S. Census lists the free inhabitants in the Low household as Andrew, Mary, Amy, Hattie, Katie, and Mary, as well as two free people of color, marked as "mulatto," Celia Anderson, age 37, and Grace Taylor, 50. Each servant listed the value of their property at $50. Andrew Low's valued $94,000. Celia Anderson also appears on Savannah's Register of Free Persons of Color for 1864. She noted her occupation as "cook," and her residency at "Drayton and Charlton," the location of the Low's rear building and carriage house. The register also states that

Mosianna and Tom Milledge, c. 1880s.

she was born in Charleston (the U.S. Census notes her birthplace as Savannah), and her required guardian as W. Cumming. In September 1865, Eliza Stiles mentions that Grace is "sewing and helping in every way," which indicates her household responsibilities. Also in 1865, Eliza Stiles wrote to her husband William Henry Stiles,

Sr., that Andrew Low employed a governess, Miss Mary McCord, for six months.

In 1844, Andrew Low purchased Tom from Wylly Woodbridge for $398.92. This man is believed to be Thomas Milledge, Low's enslaved and later free butler. Thomas married Mosianna, also an enslaved and later free servant of the Low family. Tom and Mosianna had three children, William, Thomas, Jr., and Mary. Tom sometimes accompanied Low to England. At other times, he was left in sole charge of the Low house when his owner/boss was away. Tom died in 1886. He served with the Forest City Light Infantry, and was a freemason with the Eureka Lodge No. 1. His obituary noted that "he had the respect of both white and colored people."

Later, Tom's wife Mosianna, who was twenty years younger than her husband, became the cook for Willie and Daisy Low. She may have learned her cooking skills from Celia Anderson, whose time with the Lows appears to have overlapped with Mosianna's time at the house. Mosianna Milledges's work with the younger Lows included a residency in England. Milledge is credited with teaching southern cooking to their English cook Rosa Lewis, who later became famous in London for her southern dishes. Like his parents, Thomas, Jr., also worked for the Lows. Jessie Low referred to the younger Tom as "Tommie," and described him as "a very smart funny boy."

William Makepeace Thackeray, on the enslaved children at the Andrew Low House:

"Jim and Sady are two young friends of mine at Savannah in Georgia. I made Sady's acquaintance on a first visit to America,—a pretty little brown boy with beautiful bright eyes,—and it appears that I presented him with a quarter of a dollar, which princely gift he remembered years afterwards, for never were eyes more bright and kind than the little man's when he saw me and I dined with his kind masters on my second visit. Jim, at my first visit, had been a little toddling tadpole of a creature, but during the interval of two journeys had developed into a full-blown beauty... I see him now, and Sady, and a half-dozen more of the good people, creeping on silent bare feet to the drawing-room door when the music begins, and listening with all their ears, with all their eyes. Good-night, kind, warm-hearted little Sady and Jim! May peace soon be within your walls! I have had so much kindness there, that I grieve to think of friends in arms, and brothers in anger." William Makepeace Thackeray, written in 1861 at the beginning of the Civil War as part of his "A Leaf out of a Sketch-Book" in *The Victoria Regia*, edited by Adelaide Anne Procter.

Thackeray probably referred to Jim when he made this reference in a letter to his family on his first visit to the Lows in Savannah in 1853:

"I wish you could have seen a little negrillo [sic] of five years toddling about with the plates at dinner yesterday."

John Norris, architect

John Norris (1804–1876) came to Savannah around 1845 to design and oversee the building of the United States Custom House on Bay Street, after completing the same commission in Wilmington, North Carolina. He began his career as a mason, but by 1847 the New York directory listed Norris as an architect. Although a New York native, he worked in Wilmington and Savannah from 1839 until the start of the Civil War. In Savannah, he designed dozens of buildings for both public and private use. In addition to the Custom House, his public assignments included the city's and the state's first public school (Massie), as well as the first Georgia Historical Society building, and a Unitarian church.

Andrew Low's house was his first private residence commission in the city. The Lows were friendly with the Norrises. In 1845, Sarah Low traveled with the couple in the northeast. In a letter to a friend, she noted they journeyed together from Newport, Rhode Island, to Lebanon, New York, which included a trip up the Hudson River, a stop at West Point, and a visit to the Catskill Mountains.

Opposite page: Front and rear facades
of the Andrew Low House

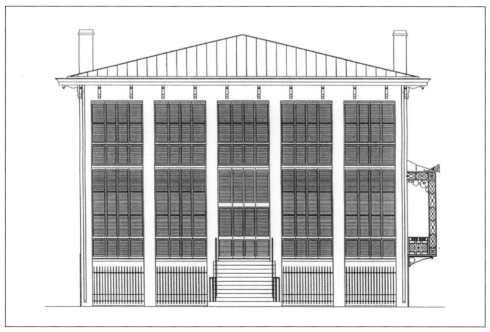

William Mackay Low and Juliette Gordon Low on their wedding day,
December 21, 1886.

Juliette "Daisy" Gordon Low

～◯⌐ Before Andrew Low died, he gave permission to his son William to marry Savannahian Juliette "Daisy" Gordon (1860–1927). Her parents also, reluctantly, allowed the engagement. The couple married on December 21, 1886, only six weeks after they buried William's father. The marriage began with a rocky start resulting from an accident on their wedding day—a grain of rice lodged in Daisy's ear, causing her great pain and permanent hearing loss.

After a short stay in Georgia, the couple left for England in the summer of 1887. Although they promised Daisy's family they would live in Savannah, the couple only returned for rare visits. Willie Low's fast lifestyle, which often excluded his wife, led to the deterioration of their marriage. The couple separated officially in 1901. Before they divorced, Willie died in 1905. The settlement of his estate favored his mistress, but Daisy received the Andrew Low House in Savannah.

In the subsequent years, Daisy spent much of her time traveling, including sojourns to Egypt and India. After she established the Girl Scouts, she dedicated her time to building the organization throughout the United States. During her visits to Savannah, she stayed with family, and rented the

Andrew Low House for income. Her tenants included poet and humorist Ogden Nash (1902–1971) who lived in the house with his family from 1908–1913. After founding the Girl Scouts, she allowed the group to use her carriage house as their headquarters, which she later left to them in her will.

Daisy died at the Andrew Low House on January 17, 1927. At 66 years of age, she succumbed to breast cancer. She left her home and garage to her nephew William Washington Gordon IV, and her brothers William Washington Gordon III, and George Arthur Gordon.

A Girl Scout troup on the steps of the Andrew Low House, c. 1922.

Top: Robert Baden-Powell, founder of the Boy Scouts, his wife
Olave Baden-Powell, Juliette Gordon Low
Bottom: Juliette Gordon Low with Girl Scouts, 1922

The National Society of The Colonial Dames of America in the State of Georgia

On January 19, 1928, The National Society of The Colonial Dames of America in the State of Georgia purchased the house from Juliette Gordon Low's family for $37,500. During the first few decades of ownership, The Georgia Dames used the house as their state headquarters. The Society hosted meetings and social gatherings on the parlor level, and used part of the basement for administrative offices. To help pay for the purchase, they rented the house for income, including a portion of the basement for a restaurant called "Colonial Kitchens," open from 1929 to 1937, and three bedrooms upstairs. In addition, on the upper floor they used a room for storage, and a space for visiting Dames. The Society opened the house for limited tours beginning in 1952, and by 1966 received visitors seven days a week.

The House
Exterior

In 1847, Andrew Low purchased Trust Lots 13 & 14, the site of the old jail, on the west side of Lafayette Square for $3,000. The following year he hired John Norris to design and build a home for his family. The house was completed in 1849. The three-story residence, including a raised basement and surrounding dry moat, is covered in scored stucco. Typical for a mid-nineteenth century home, the house presents an eclectic blending of revival styles and was especially influenced by Greek architecture.

The front entrance to the Andrew Low House makes a grand statement. Before entering the house, residents and guests must first pass between two nearly life-sized cast-iron lion sculptures guarding the staircase, climb a set of steep brownstone stairs, and step through an imposing classical entrance. The entry features a pediment and entablature supported by two brownstone fluted columns with Corinthian capitals, and two stone pilasters. Inspired by the ancient Tower of the Winds building in Athens, the columns demonstrate architect John Norris' knowledge of classical architecture. They also reference the columns he used in

his design for Savannah's U.S. Custom House.

The massive front double doors, made of wood, feature simulated studs that allude to doors from antiquity, such as the bronze exterior doors on the Temple of Romulus in Rome. Two pairs of white-painted wooden pilasters that mimic the fluted brownstone columns flank the front door. Between each set of pilasters, a narrow row of vertical windows provide light for the entrance hall. A transom, or horizontal band of windows above the doorway, brings in additional light.

Decorative cast iron balconies add an elegant, dramatic flair to the stately house. The two small uncovered balconies, painted green, flank each side of the front entrance. A longer, more elaborate covered balcony, also green, extends along the south wall.

The bracketed eaves reference Italianate designs, but the roofline was added later, after damage resulting from a hurricane in 1854. A parapet surrounded the original low-pitched metal roof.

Garden

〜◎᷾ A cast iron gate encloses the front garden, which features hour-glass shaped beds that flank the central flagstone walkway to the entrance of the house. Reproduction garden tiles border the beds. The rear garden is surrounded by a stucco covered brick wall. A pierced brick wall sets the boundary between the Andrew Low House and the Girl Scout Headquarters. The original rear garden featured a large lawn filled with camellias and osmanthus, or tea olive. Today, flagstones cover the area, and the courtyard serves as a gathering place for visitors.

Savannah Victuals

Soon after 1928, a section of the ground level, which included the old kitchen, house staff quarters, butler's pantry, and children's dining room, was converted to a tearoom, appropriately named The Colonial Kitchens, a local and regional gathering spot for several years. The menu favorites were "Beaten Biscuits," "Martha Custis Cake," and "Mrs. Habersham's Terrapin Stew."

The following excerpt by Ogden Nash, writer and humorist for the *New York Times*, was written as part of his introduction to *The Savannah Cookbook* by Georgia Dame Miss Harriet Ross Colquitt.

> "… *for as everybody knows, life on Savannah victuals*
> *is just one long round of Madeira and Skictuals*
> *…but, if you seek something headier than nectar*
> *and tastier than ambrosia and more palatable than manna,*
> *set your teeth, I beg you,*
> *in one of these spécialtiés de Savannah.*"

—V.C.L., from *Andrew Low's Legacy*

Cast iron fountain in the rear garden.

Southside "dry moat," looking towards the rear garden. Note the old lead pipe by the flower pot (above), a relic of the original plumbing system.

Interior

ᔕ With guidance from Georgia-based Edward Vason Jones in the late 1970s, the Society began furnishing the house with nineteenth-century antiques made before the Civil War. The husband of Georgia Dame Maria Martin Jones, Edward Vason Jones advised about the house's physical interpretation. Although an architect by trade, Jones fulfilled his interest in decorating and antiques by overseeing or participating in the design and furnishing of numerous public and private historic houses, including the diplomatic reception rooms at the U.S. State Department and Georgia's Governor's Mansion. His tastes leaned heavily towards the Federal period, which is reflected in the presentation at the Andrew Low House. After Jones died in 1980, his friend and colleague Berry Tracy carried forward Jones' vision. Tracy, an antiques dealer and former curator of the Metropolitan Museum of Art and Newark Museum, shared Jones' affinity for early nineteenth-century furniture. He assisted the Georgia Dames with many purchases.

Opposite:
Entrance Hall
view from the
front door

Tracy died in 1984, but the Society's work continued. A third influential person, Savannah antiques dealer Francis "Skeeter" McNairy (1943–2009), whose shop resided nearby on the corner

of Abercorn and Taylor Streets, also helped the Georgia Dames with their acquisitions.

The Society has created a historic house filled with nineteenth-century antiques carefully placed throughout the upper two floors of the building to reflect how the house would have been originally furnished and used. Over time, they have added numerous pieces that belonged to the Low family and their close relatives. They have also placed an emphasis on collecting objects originally used in Savannah and the state of Georgia.

Entrance Hall

Once inside the house, the classical architectural details continue. Plaster cornices, brackets, and ceiling centerpieces draw the eye upward, while Tower of the Winds pilasters frame the doors leading into each of the rooms on both sides of the hall, echoing exterior details. The interior doors are painted to imitate mahogany, and feature silver-plated door hardware, including knobs, face plates, key-hole covers, and hinges. On the upper floor, these fixtures are made of brass. During the redecoration project in 1979, discoveries led to the

Opposite: Entrance Hall view looking to the front door

possible identification of the builder of the house. The name "Lufburrow" was found scratched on the concealed side of a hinge on the Dining Room door, and "Thos Clark" is pressed into the hinges on the Library. Matthew Lufburrow and his partner Thomas Clark moved to Savannah from New Jersey around 1818. Their Savannah work included their homes on Oglethorpe Avenue (1821) and the Savannah Baptist Church (1830). Lufburrow is listed as a bricklayer in the 1849 city directory, and he served as Norris' foreman on the Customs House.

A classically inspired floor cloth designed by Edward Vason Jones, and made by Bob Christian, a Savannah artist, protects the floor. At the back of the hall, a staircase rises along the south wall, and forty feet from the front door, a smaller, single door opens to the rear piazza. A much smaller door, hidden under the staircase, leads to the basement. A pair of hanging lights with etched globes supported by ormolu rims provide extra light in the hall. Each lamp extends from a plaster medallion in a stylized poppy flower design, which is set into the ceiling.

The Entrance Hall would have been used to welcome guests, and serve as a passage between rooms. Reflecting this function, several chairs and a sofa are positioned against the walls. Two pier tables topped with Argand lamps, an umbrella

Convex mirror with attached candle arms, circa 1820s.

stand, a tall case clock, a pair of Chinese porcelain vases, a convex mirror with attached candle arms, and a barometer complete the hall's ensemble. In keeping with Edward Vason Jones' aesthetic tastes,

Detail: Mahogany sofa, circa 1820s.

all the furnishings in the hall date around 1820 to 1830.

Portraits of Savannahians William Taylor (1769–1840), a merchant, cotton factor, president of the St. Andrew's Society, and business associate of the Lows, and his wife Mary Elizabeth Miller Taylor (1774–1846), a quilter and founder of the Savannah Female Orphan Asylum (1801), hang by the front door. John Wesley Jarvis (1780–1840) signed the portrait of Mary Taylor, and may have painted her husband's portrait as well. Jarvis based his portrait business in New York, but spent a significant amount of time on the road, especially in the South, including Savannah. He painted large-scale paintings, standard portraits, and miniatures, of both the very well-known, such as Andrew Jackson and John Jacob Astor, as well as the men and women in the towns and cities he visited across the country. The unsigned portrait of Joseph Stiles (1758–1838), Mary Low's paternal grandfather, hangs at the rear of the hall, across from the staircase.

Double Parlor

⟋ The two doors on the right of the Entrance Hall lead to the double parlor on the north side of the house. Andrew Low's family used the Front Parlor to receive and entertain guests, while the Back Parlor was often used as a private space for the household. The pocket mahogany doors between the two parlors allowed for privacy when needed, and could be opened for larger crowds or receptions, such as New Year's Day, 1866, when Low's eldest daughters, Amy and Hattie, received thirty gentlemen callers.

Edward Vason Jones directed the restoration and furnishing plan of the parlors, including repairs to the center medallions and plaster ceilings. The matching crystal chandeliers hanging from the medallions in each parlor came from a John Norris-designed residence at 20 West Gaston Street, built in 1857. The pier mirrors in each room reflect light from the chandeliers and windows making the parlors the brightest rooms in the house. The classically inspired gilded pier mirror made by Leon Marcotte & Company of New York in 1886 in the Front Parlor was given by Juliette's parents as a wedding present for Daisy

Front Parlor

and Willie Low. The Gordons ordered two mirrors, one for the Andrew Low House, and the other for their family home on Oglethorpe Avenue. A rococo-revival gilded mirror hangs in the Back Parlor.

Jones chose the carpet pattern "Devonshire" in a Brussels weave, made in England, for both rooms. The carpet duplicated the design used for an 1840s period room at the Metropolitan Museum of Art, for which he consulted. The window treatments for both parlors feature lambrequins, or valances, made of red and gold silk lampus in a grid and rosette pattern that attach above the center of each window by an ormolu rosette. Ormolu rosettes also hold back the embroidered muslin under-curtains. Venetian blinds help control the light in the room, and are found on every period room window throughout the house.

The nearly matching couches and footstools in the Front Parlor, and armchairs in both parlors, are covered with the same fabric. Made in Boston, the couches date to the 1840s and belonged to Godfrey Barnsley (1805–1873), a cotton factor from England. Like Andrew Low, Barnsley began his career in Liverpool and immigrated to Savannah as a

Opposite: Vertical Piano, circa 1810, made by John Broadwood & Sons, in England.

teenager. He eventually became one of the wealthiest men in the South. He married Savannahian Julia Scarbrough (1810–1845) in 1828, and in 1841 moved to Cass County (now Bartow County) near his friend, Mary Low's father William Henry Stiles, Sr. Stiles owned plantations, enslaved people, and a brick yard in Savannah, as well as land in north Georgia. He was also involved in local, state, and federal politics. From 1845–1849 he served as the chargé d'affaires to Austria.

Other seating furniture on display in the parlors include a set of lyre-backed chairs, attributed to New York cabinetmaker Duncan Phyfe (1770–1854). They were acquired with the assistance of Berry Tracy. Each parlor features a pianoforte. The vertical piano in the Front Parlor was made by John Broadwood & Sons in England around 1810. The rare upright piano is made of rosewood and features elaborate bass inlay. Four tall, castor-tipped turned legs support the case, which includes a curved top to

Side chair, c.1816, attributed to Duncan Phyfe.

Ghost Story #1

Recently, a Dame had some important papers to pick up at the Low house and, since she and her companion were running later than expected, she called ahead to be sure the alarm had not been activated. After being assured that two staff members were still in a meeting, she was told to come as soon as possible before they had to leave for the day.

A short time later the two staff members heard a door open, and women's voices chatting happily. The staff assumed it was the Dame who had arrived with her friend, and they waited expectantly for the ladies to appear. Instead, the voices were heard to be drifting upstairs to the parlor floor. After a few minutes, one of the staff said that perhaps it would be polite to inform them that they were downstairs, and they walked upstairs first to the parlor floor, and then up the stairs to the bedroom floor looking for the women.

Upon reaching the bedroom floor, the voices stopped. Thinking that somehow they had missed each other, the staffers walked back down two flights of stairs. Just as they reached the ground level hallway the doorbell rang. When the Dame and her friend walked inside, they related that the staff "looked like ghosts" themselves. Indeed, they were in need of a glass of water, although something stronger probably would have been preferred! On the Girl Scout's Honor, I have repeated, as accurately as possible, this most recent encounter with our spirit friends.

—V.C.L.

protect the keyboard, and adjustable candle slides for additional lighting when needed. The lyre-shaped pedal stand references the musical purpose of the piano. A sunburst of gold silk centered with an ormolu star concealed the mechanism of the piano (now removed).

In the Back Parlor, a horizontal piano represents a more traditional instrument that probably resembles the one owned by the Lows. A & W Geib of New York made the existing piano in the early 1820s. The instrument rests on seven legs, and includes three shallow drawers with gilt bass knobs, and is decorated with ormolu mounts. The original mechanism remains intact, and is in playing condition.

The Back Parlor also includes a variety of

*Above: A nineteenth-century marble bust of Venus de Medici
Opposite: Back Parlor*

Breakfront Secretary, 1810, by Joseph Barry.
Opposite: Joseph Berry label, located under one of the interior drawers.

family-owned objects that demonstrate daily life among the leisure class. Items from the Stiles family home, Etowah Cliffs in north Georgia, include playing cards, porcelain card box, brass inlaid mahogany box, and a sculpture of two greyhounds made of a porcelain bisque material sometimes called Parian ware, which was developed in the mid-nineteenth century to simulate marble. The Stiles family also owned a set of miniature plaster casts that depicted important works of art, such as Greek and Roman statuary. Visitors touring Europe on the Grand Tour often brought

Stiles family items from their north Georgia home, Etowah Cliffs.

home these small reproductions as souvenirs. The family probably purchased their collection during their time in Austria in the mid-nineteenth century.

Although not originally owned by the family, a worktable positioned by the window at the back of the room references sewing and needlework undertaken by women of status. Created to store needles, scissors, threads, and fabric, a beautifully crafted worktable, such as this New York piece, had a utilitarian purpose, but also made a statement about the owner who could afford such a specific piece of furniture.

Situated against the south wall stands the most important piece of furniture in the collection, a breakfront secretary originally owned by Robert

Toy blocks once belonging to the Stiles family.

Mackay (1772–1816), a wealthy merchant in Savannah and Liverpool and Mary Low's maternal grandfather. Made by Joseph Barry (1757?–1838), as indicated on the label located on an interior drawer, the piece commands the room. Barry, an Irish immigrant who settled in Philadelphia, took refuge in Savannah from the yellow fever epidemic in Philadelphia in 1798. He advertised his wares for sale at the "Mein's and Mackay's Stores under the Bluff," and maintained a long relationship with this firm for years after his brief stay in Savannah. This connection resulted in Robert Mackay's acquisition of the 1810 breakfront secretary. Made with high-end woods, including mahogany, rosewood, amaranth, satinwood, and tulip, and first-rate craftmanship, the case serves as an important specimen of early nineteenth century American cabinetmaking. The central bookcase doors present a Gothic tracery, while the exterior doors each display a fifteen-paned geometric pattern. A fall-front panel revels the interior secretary made of satinwood. Two of the small drawers hide secret compartments. Barry advertised this specialty add-on, which he called "secrets." Floating sections in the shape of ovals and squares with inset corners accentuate the matching mahogany veneers on the exterior cabinet doors. Six beehive-turned feet, and two tapered square feet (not

Amethyst jewelry, first owned by Napoleon's second wife, Marie Louise, the Duchess of Parma, and later purchased by William Henry Stiles for his wife Eliza.

visible), support the massive case.

Perhaps the most important family-related objects in the house are the portraits of Andrew Low, and the two portraits of his second wife Mary. The portrait of Andrew Low hangs over the mantle in the Front Parlor (see page 11). Painted by the Philadelphia artist George Washington Conarroe (1801–1882), the picture depicts the twenty-four-year old on the eve of a successful career. Conarroe painted Low's portrait in late 1836 during a brief "professional visit" to Savannah where he offered his portrait painting services.

Conarroe painted the young, red-headed Andrew Low holding a stack of papers (on which Conarroe signed his name), indicating his position as a businessman. Low appears serious, but friendly, as he gazes at the viewer.

The two portraits of Mary Low depict the newlywed in three-quarter view. The larger oil on canvas portrait hanging over the mantle in

An Earlier Restoration

Around 1950, Franco Scalamandré heard about the Andrew Low House from a friend in Charleston, James Leath, an interior decorator who had been asked to help restore the house interiors. Leath invited Mr. Scalamandré and another decorator, Nancy McClelland, known as one of the most outstanding designers of authentic French and American historic wallpapers, to share with him the gratification of properly decorating it. With much enthusiasm, both agreed to assist in restoring the Andrew Low House to its former dignified elegance.

Indeed, not only did Mr. Scalamandré provide beautiful silk hangings from his well-known line of exquisite fabrics, Mrs. McClelland recruited one of Savannah's most respected architects, John Lebey, to assist on the project. Lebey, an architect for the historic site commission, made beautiful drawings and sent pictures via the U.S. Postal Service to expedite the work. Interesting how times have changed!

According to the *Savannah Morning News*, April 16, 1950, "After many telephone conversations among the 'Famous Four,' once more the century-old Low house became a thing of beauty." —V.C.L.

the Back Parlor was painted by an unknown artist. Mary, pictured here in her early twenties, holds a flower in one hand, and touches a bouquet of flowers on the table with her other hand. This formal portrait, which depicts Mary Low in a brilliant blue dress with lace collar and sleeves, renders a confident woman easily identifiable in fine parlors such as

Andrew Low's. The smaller pastel on the easel in the Front Parlor closely resembles the larger painting. In both portraits, Mary Low wears the same dress (with a few variations), holds a similar pose and gaze, and wears the same hair style. The pastel portrait was created in Paris by Fredericks Penabert & LeBlance (working 1854–1857) during the Low's honeymoon in 1854. The most striking difference in the two paintings is the lack of a wedding ring on Mary's hand in the oil portrait.

Brooch with seed pearls and garnets, a wedding gift from Robert E. Lee to Eliza Mackay Stiles, 1832.

Library

⟊⟎ᵐ The Library is located across the Entrance
Hall from the Front Parlor. Andrew Low likely used
this small chamber as his home office. The room
is furnished in a fashion suited for such purposes.
Daisy Low referred to this space as the "Smoking
Room," which indicates the purpose of the room
during the time she and Willie lived in the house.

The decoration includes a Brussels-woven carpet
in the "Lorenzo" pattern, reproduced by Hugh
Mackay & Company in Durham, England, after

a carpet found in the 1807 neoclassical Lorenzo mansion in Cazenovia, New York. Reproduced by the Guenther Wood Group in 1994, three French-polished mahogany pelmets, or cornice boards, with ormolu mounts top each window. A red silk valance hangs from each support, which frames sheer Swiss voile curtains. Historic red and green tassels made of silk hang from gilt metal tiebacks with a stylized floral pattern. The tassels came from The Hermitage, an 1820 Savannah area mansion and plantation, now demolished. The plantation functioned as an industrial site where enslaved people ran rice mills, sugar works, an iron foundry, and made bricks for construction through-out the city, including the Andrew Low House.

A secretary between the front windows, and a row of bookcases along the north wall anchor the room. Two classically inspired busts sit atop the bookcases. Made of Parian ware, the busts add a touch of elegance to the otherwise masculine space. Between the busts, hanging on the wall, is a portrait of Robert Toombs (1810–1885). Toombs, a slaveholding planter, was active in politics in the state of Georgia. He served in the Georgia state legislature, as well as the United States Congress, both as a Representative and Senator. During the Civil War, he briefly served in the military, and as the Confederacy's Secretary of State.

The mahogany and satinwood secretary dates to the second quarter of the nineteenth century, and originally resided in the Clanton home in Augusta, Georgia. A swivel desk chair, armchair, and rocking chair represent three different seating styles from the first half of the nineteenth century. The room also includes a Canterbury, used to hold sheet music, card table, clock, and a pair of Argand lamps. Overhead, a three-branched bronze Argand chandelier extends from a ceiling medallion designed by Edward Vason Jones. Argand lamps used a sleeve-shaped wick, burned whale or vegetable oil, and created a light source up to ten times brighter than one candle.

Situated on the secretary and card table, original and reproduction family portraits bring the house to life. Two images depict Andrew Low's first wife, Sarah Cecil Hunter, and daughter Amy, and his second wife, Mary Stiles, as a young woman. Signed "C. Durham, 1849," the small watercolor on ivory portrait of Sarah and Amy Low portray both mother and child wearing typical mid-nineteenth century clothing in tartan patterns, reflecting the couple's Scottish ancestry. The colorful blues in Sarah Low's dress, and the velvet book on her lap, are especially brilliant. Sarah Low's piercing, straightforward gaze gives the picture a haunting impression, perhaps heighted by the knowledge she died shortly after this

Portrait of William Mackay Low, circa 1897, by James Linwood Palmer.

painting was rendered. Vivid blues were also uti-
lized in the watercolor portrait of the young Mary
Cowper Stiles. This picture is believed to have
been painted by her mother Eliza Mackay Stiles.

Finally, an oil on canvas portrait of Willie Low,
age 37, astride Rightaway, hangs over the fireplace.
Painted by the British equestrian artist James
Linwood Palmer (1868–1941), who specialized in
depicting lively race horses, the picture features
a mud-splattered Low in his hunting attire on
an animal in motion. A well-known sportsman
in England, Low had dozens of award-winning
horses stabled at Wellesbourne House, his home
in Warwickshire.

Butler's Pantry

The small passage between the Library and Dining Room provided access to the Butler's Pantry (now closed off for a Docent lounge), and steep staircase that led to the upper and lower floors. This staircase would have been used by the Low children and Tom and Mosianna Milledge, as well as all the other servants who worked at the house.

Recollection of an incident involving Tom Milledge *by John Mackay Elliot, Mary Low's cousin*

"That summer [1865] I helped my Aunt Eliza Stiles and guarded the house where she and a governess cared for her grandchildren while their wealthy English father Andrew Low was away. Their mother had died and, Savannah being in a turmoil, I often prowled around the house at night as the dark was filled with alarms and excursions. One night the dog made such a racket that I took my revolver and crept downstairs and lit the gas in the entrance hall. Approaching the front door, I saw with horror the knob of the closed library door silently turn. I took good aim at whoever was opening it—then it came to me, what a terrible thing it would be to kill a man like that, and I cried, 'Who's there?' 'Me, sir, Tom,' the faithful Negro coachman who, hearing the alarm of the dog, had entered the house with a key unknown to me."

Tom Milledge probably entered the house from the basement and came up the back stairs through the Butler's Pantry, then the Library when he encountered John Elliot.

Opposite: Back stairs between the library and dining room.

Dining Room

∿☉⁾ʷ· With easy access to the kitchen via the stairs in the adjacent passage, and the dumbwaiter in the Butler's Pantry, John Norris situated the Dining Room on the southwest side of the main floor. Edward Vason Jones chose the paint color for this room, and oversaw the restoration of the center medallion and plaster ceiling. Berry Tracy oversaw the rest of the installation. For the window treatments, Tracy followed a design by the nineteenth-century French decorator Pierre de La Mésangère (1761–1831). For the Brussels-woven carpet, Tracy continued the "Lorenzo" pattern from the Library into the Dining Room. The four-armed gilt-bronze chandelier in a rococo revival style features four Parian ware bellflowers. The light fixture was possibly made by Cornelius & Company of Philadelphia.

The room is furnished with all the appropriate accoutrements necessary for a nineteenth-century dining room, including an expandable center table, side tables, and a sideboard. The center table belonged to Robert Mackay. He also once owned the painting of a ship in three views that now hangs on the east wall. Launched in St. Mary's, Georgia, in 1801, *General Oglethorpe* made one voyage to England. On her return trip, she stopped in

Charleston, and then wrecked somewhere around the Bahamas in 1802. Twenty-three men died in the accident, but Mackay, two slaves, and seven other men survived at sea for twelve days before their rescue by a passing schooner. During *General Oglethorpe*'s brief stay in England, Mackay commissioned the noted marine artist Robert Salmon (1775–1845) to paint the ship. The painting hung over the sideboard in the Mackay home on Broughton Street for many years. Mackay's great-great-grandson William Mills donated the picture, and many other Mackay family items, to the Andrew Low House.

Sitting atop the table is a partial dinner service attributed to the makers Dihl et Guérhard (French, 1781-c. 1824). Created in the early nineteenth-century for an American market, a thirteen-star America flag is depicted on each plate. All examples contain classical and allegorical images relating to agriculture, music, war, and commerce. The Metropolitan Museum of Art holds other pieces from this service in its collection.

The chairs around the table and the room originally belonged to Godfrey Barnsley. The Georgia Dames own twenty of the original twenty-four chairs. The Society acquired the chairs, and a few other objects that belonged to Barnsley, through Scarbrough descendants. The New York-made

*Three views of Robert Mackay's ship General Oglethorpe,
1801, by Robert Salmon.*

chairs date to the 1820s and replicate the ancient
Greek klismos form, which features scroll-back
decoration and front and rear saber legs that splay
outward in a concave fashion, much like the
curve of a sword.

Used for storage and display, the sideboard was
an important feature of the dining room. The
Andrew Low House sideboard dates to about 1820.
Made in New York, the large piece of furniture
features mahogany veneers, bass ormolu elements,
and gilded sections. Ionic columns and acanthus

Robert Mackay's silver-mounted and carved coconut shell, 1797–1798.
Opposite: Other examples of silver on display in the Dining Room.

leaf-covered feet, create a stately, but elegant piece that references classical architecture. On the wall, above the sideboard, hangs a portrait of Jessie Low Graham, Andrew and Mary Low's youngest child. Created in about 1895, the painting is attributed to Charles Alexander Smith (1864–1915), a Canadian artist known to have painted other portraits of the Graham family.

Various examples of silver hollowware sit atop the sideboard, displayed to appropriately mimic the original use of the furniture. Most of the silver in this room and throughout the house was acquired through various Georgia Dames and have

Above: The early nineteenth-century étegere displays a number of period objects. A chair once owned by Godfrey Barnsley sits nearby. Opposite: Several pieces of the Stiles family red Bohemian glass dessert service, 1849.

some connection to Savannah or the state. A few pieces belonged to Mary Low's family, including her grandfather Robert Mackay's silver-mounted carved coconut shell, 1797–1798, and a silver salver made by London silversmith Robert Abercrombie in 1743.

The red Bohemian glass displayed on the pier table between the west windows represent a larger service purchased by Mary Low's parents in 1849. William and Eliza Stiles purchased a dessert set of

Examples of the partial dinner service made by Dihl et Guérhard, early nineteenth century.

144 pieces during William's time serving his diplomatic post in Austria. The original service included candlesticks, decanters, wine glasses, plates and saucers of different sizes, and an epergne—a centerpiece used for holding and displaying food and

Salver, 1743, made by Robert Abercrombie, and descended through the Mackay family.

flowers. Each piece featured red glass cut to clear in the form of grapes, leaves, and vines. Additionally, nearly every piece included the engraved initials "WHS". The Andrew Low House now owns eleven pieces, acquired from Stiles family descendants. At Christmas, the house exhibits the set on the dining room table.

The Upper Floor

〰️〽️ The Upper Floor includes five bedrooms, a bathing room, a sizable hall, and an enclosed passage with access to the back staircase. Like the parlor level, members of the Georgia Society filled the bedrooms with period furnishings and reproduction decorations. They named each bedroom by someone who either lived in or visited the house.

The northwest bedroom was designated the Robert E. Lee Beroom. Lee stayed at the house as Andrew Low's guest in April 1870, purportedly in this room. Lee's long-term friendship with the family began in 1829 when he came to Savannah at the age of twenty-two as a recent graduate of the U. S. Military Academy at West Point. Lee served as an engineer and assisted with the planning, design, and management of the early preparation and construction of a fort on Cockspur Island, today's Fort Pulaski. While in Savannah, he spent a significant amount of time with the Mackay

Main stairs to the Upper Floor.

Robert E. Lee Bedroom

Gaslights

The Savannah Gas Company was not organized until January 15, 1850, and it was not until the end of August, after the city contract was approved, that there was an order to proceed with gas piping for city streets only. Andrew Low II was on this particular city board, and one can only imagine his cautious optimism with such advancement to the creature comforts in Savannah.　　—V.C.L.

family. Lee attended West Point with their son Jack, Mary Low's maternal uncle. Later, in 1886, Willie Low stayed in this room when he returned from England for his father's funeral and his own wedding.

The Society designated the center room on the north side of the floor as the Children's Bedroom. When William Makepeace Thackeray visited in 1856, he wrote about a baby "crowing in the adjoining nursery." Members of the Georgia Society have filled the room with two beds, and nineteenth-century toys. The pale green painted furniture, which include four pieces—a bed, chest of drawers, dressing table, and bedside table, originally furnished a room at the Johnston-Felton-

Painted bedroom furniture originally from the Johnston-Felton-Hay House in Macon, now in the Children's Bedroom.
Opposite: Second floor hall.

An English settee, c. 1810, rests against the north wall, between the Thackeray and Children's Bedrooms. The Sheraton style settee is painted black with gilt stenciled bands on the slightly curved backs. There are four conforming seating sections within the two end arms. The front legs are turned and the seat is cane with a drop-cushion covered in a gold and white striped satin. Traditionally, this settee would have been the "post" for two maiden aunts to sit upon while acting as chaperones during social events occurring on the first floor. Fully familiar with the invitation list, they would keep a watchful Victorian eye on any unmarried couples advancing to the second floor and maintain a proper decorum enforcing the bedroom-door-open and bathing-room-door-closed policy. The aunts would do this with such engaging aplomb that any young couple would be none the wiser. —V.C.L.

Painted bedroom furniture in the Children's Bedroom

Hay House in Macon. The smaller walnut bed originally belonged to the Barnsleys at Woodlands, in north Georgia.

The front, northeast room is named for William Makepeace Thackeray (1811–1863). The British author lodged with Andrew Low while on speaking tours in 1853 and 1856. He described the home as "the most comfortable quarters I have ever had in the United States."

The rosewood writing desk that sits between the front two windows is the only piece of furniture from Andrew Low's era that remains in the house. Oral history accounts suggest the secretary resided in this room when Thackeray visited. The roll-topped desk is attributed to New Jersey cabinetmaker John Jelliff (1813–1893). Made in a rococo revival style with cabriole legs, and ornate pierced gallery, the compact writing desk provides a pleasant and adequate surface in which to pen letters or compose literature.

The majestic Jamaican-made mahogany four-poster bed that takes up most of the space in the room was a wedding gift to Robert and Eliza McQueen Mackay in 1800, given by Eliza's aunt Mary Smith (1751–1821) and her husband Basil Cowper (d. 1802). British sympathizers, the Cowpers escaped to Jamaica after the Revolutionary War. Mary Cowper Stiles Low was named

Above: Rosewood writing desk attributed to John Jelliff is believed once used by William Makepeace Thackeray.

Opposite: Mahogany four-poster bed, made in Jamaica, a wedding gift to Robert and Eliza McQueen Mackay from Eliza's aunt and uncle Mary and Basil Cowper.

Bathing Room

after the Cowper's daughter Mary (d. 1856) who lived with Eliza Mackay in the later years of her life. The serpentine-shaped tester frames a sunburst-styled insert, which is gathered under a mahogany finial (not pictured).

Located on the east wall, across the hall from the staircase, is the reproduced Bathing Room. Although indoor bathrooms existed in the United States from the first part of the nineteenth-century, this interior luxury remained available only to the wealthiest people well into the early twentieth century. The reconstructed cabinet for the tub and enclosed chamber pot is based upon structural remnants, as well as other existing examples and period documents. The 1848 copper tub came from the Hunt-Phelan House in Memphis, Tennessee. The French-born and -trained, New York–based cabinetmaker Alexander Roux (1813–1886) made the shaving stand. Two entrances to the Bathing Room originally existed, one from the current hall door, and the other to the southwest bedroom, now known as the Low Bedroom.

Plumbing at the house included a complex system of concealed gutters, which led to a large cistern buried in the back garden. A pump transferred water to the cistern in the attic, which led to the bathing room, the sink in the Butler's Pantry, and likely to the kitchen in the basement.

Used as the master bedchamber, the Low Bedroom is named for the two people who used this room the most, Andrew and Mary Low. The room is also the location where Daisy Low resided in the later years of her life and the room in which she died. Originally loaned by Edward Vason Jones

Ghost Story #2

Not too long ago, two dependable docents had a rare slow day due to inclement weather. One of the docents decided to make rounds throughout the house to get a little exercise, pass the time, and insure everything was in its proper place. From the moment she reached the top of the stairs on the second floor, she sensed something strange and out of place. She glanced around the bedrooms, but noticed nothing wrong. Shifting her focus to the bathing room, she realized the bathing room chair was sitting in the middle of the floor, not in its usual location. Naturally she assumed the other docent had reason to move it during a tour, so she shifted it back to its usual location. She then proceeded downstairs and asked her counterpart if she had moved the chair in the bathing room to the center of the room. She emphatically replied, "Absolutely not!" Both docents returned to the second floor together, and saw that the chair was once again in the middle of the room. The docents cheerfully determined that the chair must want to be the center of attention in the bathing room; however, they proceeded to move it back to its proper position. Then they turned on their heels, shut off the lights, locked up, and left—and the mystery remains unsolved! —V.C.L.

Low Bedroom

and later purchaed for the museum, the New York–
made bed dates to the early nineteenth century
and features reeded posts with carved acanthus
leaves that sit on brass-capped feet with castors. A
worktable sits at the foot of the bed, which indicates a female presence. The dressing table by the
window, and the bureau (not pictured) represent

Eliza Mackay Stiles Bedroom, featuring portraits of family members.

the type of furniture used by a married couple in the mid-nineteenth century.

The southwest room, called the Eliza Mackay Stiles Bedroom, denotes the space where Mary Low's mother Eliza stayed after her daughter's death in 1863. Later, Daisy and Willie Low made this their master bedchamber, adjacent to a newer attached bathroom on the back piazza (no longer existing).

This room includes a few pieces connected to Savannah, including the Mackay family crib. The large mahogany wardrobe (not pictured) belonged to John Macpherson Berrien (1781–1856). Berrien, whose house sits on the northwest corner of Broughton and Habersham Streets, served twice as a U.S. Senator, and as a U.S. Attorney General under Andrew Jackson. Berrien's wife Eliza Cecil Hunter was the first cousin of Sarah Cecil Hunter Low.

The wash stand positioned on the northeast wall by the window was made in Massachusetts, circa 1830. This unique piece could also be used as a dressing table, and is noteworthy for the cutout openings on the top surface used to accommodate a large set of porcelain toiletries, such as a washing bowl, pitchers, soap and sponge dishes, and mugs. Additionally, the back compartment between the pedestal support hides the double-hinged, adjustable mirror when not needed.

Like many of the other rooms in the house, this bedroom displays a number of family images. On the north wall, three watercolors of the Stiles family—Eliza Stiles and two of her three children Mary Low, and William Henry Stiles, Jr.—hang opposite an engraving of Eliza's husband and their children's father William Henry Stiles, Sr. Below his portrait is a framed drawing by Katie Low, the eldest daughter of Andrew and Mary, made when she was ten years old. Hanging over the mantel is an oil on canvas portrait of Caroline Steenbergen Gordon, the wife of George Gordon, Juliette Gordon Low's uncle. Created the year of their marriage, 1850, the sitter only lived one year after the creation of this portrait.

Basement (not on public view)

～〇''' Originally the basement included the kitchen, laundry room, children's dining room, and quarters for the enslaved and free servants. Today, the space is used for administrative purposes. The Society has plans to reconstruct the kitchen in effort to broaden their interpretation of the site, like the restoration of the bathing room on the upper floor. In addition to restoring important areas of the house, The Georgia Dames continue to place importance on preserving the site and collections. Like The National Society, The Georgia Dames take seriously Article II of their National constitution, which states, in part:

> *The objects of this Society shall be to collect and preserve manuscripts, traditions, relics, and mementos of bygone days; to preserve and restore buildings connected with the early history of our country; to educate our fellow citizens and ourselves in our country's history and thus diffuse healthful and intelligent information concerning the past.*

Suggested Reading

Abbott, James A., et al. *Classical to 19th Century America: The Influence of Berry Tracy on the Historic Interior*. Garrison, New York: Boscobel Restoration, 1994.

Cordery, Stacy A. *Juliette Gordon Low: The Remarkable Founder of the Girl Scouts*. New York, New York: Viking Penguin, 2012.

Farnham, Katharine G. "Classicism Returns to Georgia: Shaping a Collection of American Federal Period Furniture for the Governor's Mansion in Atlanta." In *Decorative Arts in Georgia: Historic Sites, Historic Context*. Athens, Georgia: Georgia Museum of Art, 2008.

Harris, Leslie M., and Daina Ramey Berry. *Slavery and Freedom in Savannah*. Athens, Georgia: University of Georgia Press, 2014.

Logan, Virginia Connerat *Andrew Low's Legacy*. published by The National Society of The Colonial Dames of America in the State of Georgia, 2016. https://www.scribd.com/document/1513497111/Andrew-Low-Legacy

Mitchell, William R. *Edward Vason Jones 1909–1980: Architect, Connoisseur, and Collector*. Savannah, Georgia: Golden Coast Publishing Company, 1995.

Morrison, Mary Lane. *John S. Norris: Architect in Savannah, 1846–1860.* Savannah, Georgia: The Beehive Press, 1980.

Ryan, Jennifer Guthrie and Hugh Stiles Golson. *Andrew Low and the Sign of the Buck: Trade, Triumph, Tragedy at the House of Low.* Savannah, Georgia: Frederic C. Beil, 2011.

Sammons, Tania June. "Feeling Gravity's Pull: The Andrew Low House Bathing Room, A Mid-Nineteenth-Century Example." In *Georgia Inside & Out: Architecture, Landscape, and Decorative Arts.* Athens, Georgia: Georgia Museum of Art, 2004.

Sammons, Tania. "Pioneers in Historic Preservation," *The Magazine Antiques.* July, 2007.

Talbott, Page. *Classical Savannah: Fine & Decorative Arts, 1800–1840.* Savannah, Georgia: Telfair Museum of Art, 1995.

Theus, Mrs. Charlton M. *Savannah Furniture, 1735–1825.* Savannah, Georgia: Privately printed, 1967.

Weinraub, Anita Zaleski, ed. *Georgia Quilts: Piecing Together a History.* Athens, Georgia: University of Georgia Press, 2006.

Publication of this book was supported, in part,
by the Kenneth Coleman Series in Georgia History and Culture.

Published by the University of Georgia Press
Athens, Georgia 30602
www.ugapress.org
© 2018 by The National Society of The Colonial Dames
of America in the State of Georgia

Photography by Richard Leo Johnson
Design by Pinafore Press / Janice Shay
Additional photography by Charlie Ribbens: pages 43, 44, 52
and James Gibbons, Jr.: page 8

Coordination Committee:
Mrs. Paul Moffatt Pressly,
Chairman of the Savannah Town Committee
Mrs. Nolan Cordill Moore,
Chairman of the Andrew Low House Board
Mrs. Joy Daniels Schwartz,
NSCDA-GA President
Mr. Stephen Bohlin,
Executive Director of the Andrew Low House

Printed and bound by Thomson-Shore
The paper in this book meets the guidelines for permanence
and durability of the Committee on Production Guidelines for
Book Longevity of the Council on Library Resources.

Most University of Georgia Press titles are
available from popular e-book vendors.

Printed in the United States of America
18 19 20 21 22 C 5 4 3 2 1

Library of Congress Control Number: 2017960060
ISBN: 9780820353982 (hardcover: alk. paper)